Meraki

A dreamer's journey

Tavisshi

First Published in October 2021

ISBN:978-93-5472-550-0

BLUEROSE PUBLISHERS

www.bluerosepublishers.com

info@bluerosepublishers.com

+91 8882 898 898

Cover Design:

Mukti Verma

Typographic Design:

Jyoti Sharma

Distributed by: BlueRose, Amazon, Flipkart

To my mom, dad, dadu, dadi, nanu and nani

None of this would have happened if it weren't for you

To the readers

It is for you I put this out in the world

INDEX

"At the touch of love

everyone becomes a poet"

~Plato

FORWARD

To be honest writing a book had never really been a dream of mine but as I write this, I realize I have no words to describe how I truly feel right now. This book is the result of countless hours of writing and late nights of editing. Poetry to me has always been my way of expression; it is something that bears my soul, creativity and all my love, which led me to write 'Meraki'. It depicts the emotions that have been talked about in this book and how doing something with such devotion or putting apart of yourself into your work can birth such magnificent results. I haven't always been good at writing in fact for a long time I used to dread writing anything, until one day when I read a simple poem on the internet about the sun which struck the match for my first poem 'fire'

As human beings we have the capability of feeling a multitude of emotions, as we grow older we might not remember everything that happened in our life, but what we always remember is how we felt in that moment, the emotions we felt; happiness, anger, confusion, excitement, love. Each and every one of them is so intricate in their own self.

My intent with Meraki is for you to be able to view the world through another person's perspective. To see the very emotions you feel from someone else's eyes. This book is a journey of self-realization, love, heartbreak, rebellion, content and lastly and most importantly happiness.

Purple Hyacinths

Drowning
Why
Locked inside
Chased
Love notes
The bad guys
To feel lonely
Should I smile or cry?
My demons
Who is it really?
Pick me

"There is way too much hurt
in such a fragile body"

the ice under my feet is cracking ever so slightly
every step i take every move i make is a different rush, a thrill
at last it shatters, into small diminutive pieces
the water inside engulfs my body in a cold coerced hug
the cold water is biting at my face, nibbling up my gentle skin
as i go in deeper my body gets heavier, like a weight is pulling me down
my mind has separated itself from my body
i push myself up and aim towards the light right above my head
i try to reach it, strike my hand up but the light moves away
gradually i sink in deeper, my body feels paralysed, mind numb
the light has now scattered into a million tiny pieces
every single one is as bright as a star on a dark night
languidly those stars have faded away
i am drowning so deep my chest hurts
every thought is like a battle; every breath is like a war
the demons inside are controlling me now
i try but they just don't go away
they are pulling me down, the thoughts, the sadness
i am drowning deeper into this fathomless abyss
i am drowning but nobody sees my struggle
i am shouting but nobody hears a sound
time and death shall depart now
as my soul escaped and found a way to keep living
it is now i realise for life and death are one
even as the river and sea are one.

{*Drowning*}

why is it
that i have to go through a lifetime of hell
to get the tiniest taste of heaven.
{*Why*}

i heard a slight click
i am locked inside this room
the door is jammed shut, the window lock broken
i try to jerk it open but it wont budge
i try to yell for help but i am all alone
tired and weary i stumble to the ground
the moon outside is shining bright
it's faint light shining through the window
bouncing off my skin, glittering on my gown
i don't know how long i have been here
a fear creeps up my back
what if no one finds me
my breath caught in my throat, refusing to escape
i cutch the emerald green fabric covering me
the shadows in the shifting light scare me
what if i am left forgotten and forsaken
my fingers begin to ache and knuckles go white
i lean my head against the bedpost
and look up at the ceiling,
the plain walls, a mirror hanging crookedly on one side
the painting of a sunset on the other
a tiny lamp near the bare bed
oh it's been so long
the walls seem to close in
air being sucked out through an invisible hole
sweat dripping down the back of my neck
strands of hair stuck to my temples

i try to stand but my knees buckle
the room starts spinning, i feel suffocated
tears of fear and pain are streaming down my face
i thud onto the heavy door screaming for help
scratching the wood, scraping off the paint
my fingers bleed, going numb from the pain
i crumble to the floor, my hot cheek
touching the cool wooden floor beneath me
with my tear stained cheek and blood soaked hand
i close my eyes as i wait
for someone to break through and save me.
{*Locked inside*}

i was running away
barrelling through the damp woods
he is still following me
glaring at me with his bloodthirsty eyes
twigs and dead leaves snapping under my feet
my brown hair bouncing up my back
my skirt covered in mud
boots slipping on the soaked ground
i know he is still behind me
the way he wears the smell of blood
and death like a perfume
i look back to steal a glance at him
oh… how he had the face of an angel
but the mind of a killer
i drag myself forward trying to not give in
i fix my eyes on the moon, how the trees scatter its light
it shines as if light passing
through broken windowpanes
he is getting closer i can feel it
i slip…
i stumble to the ground and hit an old apple tree
i compel myself to get up, a twig tearing my skirt
i run as fast as i can
blood from my wound streaming down my shoulder
i see some light afar i am near the end
and soon night turns to day
and trees turn to grass, i escaped
i let out a breath i didn't know i was holding
i relax the muscles i didn't know were tensed
weary and wounded i plummet to the ground

soaking in all the sunlight
a twig snapped behind me
is he still there?
{*Chased*}

write down your love to me
on a note
cause at least paper never forgets.
{*Love notes*}

why do you only see their story?
the good guys
the ones who made all the write decisions
selfless
brave
good
one who chooses to die
rather than side with the devil
pathetic
why not us?
why not the other side?
the ones who lost
they do say the villain had a bad past
pushed to the limits
that he took matters in his own hands
"but you were the one who supported him
chose to side with evil and work for him"
haven't they ever seen the story from our side?
don't they know that sometimes
you don't have a choice between right and wrong
you don't get to choose between good or bad
the only choice you get is between wrong and death
and this is what separates us from them right?
one is selfish enough to leave and die
and the other is selfless enough to live on
perhaps they would never see our side
but then again, we are the bad guys
right?

{*The bad guys*}

loneliness has that hushed voice
the sound no one seems to hear
the sound of an empty house
the dinner table set for one
the voice of a busy station
where people simply come and go
not looking up, when life has a show
the voice of a falling tear
the feeling of nothing but despair
but maybe the voice can be a prayer

loneliness has a colour
a colour that's not quite white
the colour of a hazy night
when doing nothing feels just right
the colour of burning ash
when everything seems to be in a void
the colour of a dark storm
while the warrior of the light fights.
{*To feel lonely*}

you always smile
like you're about to cry
i can't tell which
would cause me more pain
continuing to smile
or letting yourself cry
i think the first, you say
to hide your emotions
it's never easy
to not do what you wish to
and to weather the torment
without blinking an eye
but that's where you're wrong
she told me

if i do let myself cry
that would be the end
to acknowledge the anguish
building within me
would simply be too painful to bear
i would implode
all the positivity gone from me
what would be left?
a gaping hole inside my chest
just waiting to be the end of me
no light could escape
only the darkness would remain
and the darkness is simply too dark
so i smile instead
a smile that only feeds

into the darkness
because if i don't smile
i will surely cry.
{*Should I smile or cry?*}

you can never get
rid of your demons
just like humans
they adapt
and they change.
{*My demons*}

is it monsters that make war?
or
is it war that makes monsters?
is it the people that are filled with poison?
the poison that seeps in the ground beneath their feet
and turns that very ground into a battlefield
people who speak the language of greed, bloodlust and anger
people who destroy worlds for pleasure
the ones who drink blood like it's the finest of red wine
or is it perhaps war?
the war that fills them up with poison
a war continuing from the start of times
war that destroys the good inside the person so much
that they have nothing left but darkness
war that fills the air with deception, betrayal and fraud
war that never ends itself but everything around it
it took me long enough to realize
how wrong i really was
there is no question of or
it is war that makes monsters and
monsters that make war
it is as simple as that.
{*Who is it really?*}

i love myself

and yet

i want to be wanted.

{*Pick me*}

Red Roses

Hypnotic eyes
A world of difference
Beating hearts
Till death do us apart
I love you
Crazy in love
Dreamers
In love with a monster
Abnormal
Is it enough?
Paramour
Meaning of love
Skinny love
Perfections

"Two souls are sometimes created together
and in love before they're even born."

i can’t tell
if i’m lost in your eyes
or if i'm just lost.
{*Hypnotic eyes*}

i was alone yet brave at heart
you were just and loyal and that set us apart
us together would be like oil fire and gasoline
hurt heads and hearts in a shatter
how do we know if there is a bond to break?
there is nothing there if there's no step we take
there would be a new revelation every day
the long nights and fun games through which we all stay
the vows we are resistant to break
the smiles we say we'll never fake
have to make it through for you to see
that your lone heart belongs to me
i want to tell you something now without a shadow of doubt
to think you are with me nothing makes me more proud
together or apart i will always care
doesn't matter where we are i will always be there.

{A world of difference}

how stupid are humans?
they try to control hearts
when hearts exist only to be
wild, untamed and beautiful.
{*Beating hearts*}

i never thought i would need love
but when i met you i couldn't help but fall
we have grown together, hand in hand
in you i find solace, i find my home
we may not live to see our glory
but i will join you in the fight
and when our children will tell the story,
they will tell the story of tonight
the two star crossed lovers
they loved each other not for their body but for their soul
millions of people to meet before they died
but what they chose was each other
it was unfair to bring death unto such young mortals
they didn't cry or weep, just held each other close
until their very last moment, they didn't let go
they gazed at each other, their last words being
till death do us part.
{*Till death do us apart*}

i love you
i love you
i love you
i love you
how many more times
till i start believing too.
{*I love you*}

i love you so much
so why would you do this?
blood-soaked hands, torn shirt
and dazed he stood in front of me
"why?" i ask again
hands shaking, mouth dry, knees frozen
a dead man on the floor
"for you." he said
all of it just for you
i feel the fear engulfing me
fear of him and fear for him
because i can still see
behind the bloodlust and the anger
the eyes of the innocent man
the one i fell in love with
the calm, naïve man
who loved beyond measure
his love so passionate, so fierce
oh! how it changed him
he felt so unworthy, not enough
the passion turned to anger
the fierceness took over him
and turned those eyes
those gentle grey eyes
into cold grey, fathomless eyes
i would burn the world for you
he says, his voice filled with love
dear lord!
i would never let anyone tear us apart
his hand on my tear stained cheek

i feel safe again
safe in the hands of a killer
i try not to give in
stop it...
my voice trembles
i did this all for you!
he shouted, rage and love mixed in his voice
i never asked for it
he looks at me as if betrayed, deceived
you are not the man i loved
i hold his ice-cold face
but if he is still there
desperately reaching my love
i love you so much.
{*Crazy in love*}

i don't dream as much
when i'm with you
because i already have
everything i want, in my arms.
{*Dreamers*}

you are in love with a monster
they all said to me
i never believed them
"oh, how blind could you be?
look at him"
that ravenous look
those crazy eyes
those lips that never smile
the mouth that only curses
that body with those hideous scars
he is not like any of us
"how could you possibly love him?"
those words resonate in my mind
because they don't seem true at all
because when i see him all i can see
is a look of desperate longing
eyes filled with love and passion
a smile that lights up the whole world
words filled with compassion and endearment
the scars he bears tell stories
of his tremendous will
then why is there a difference?
why does he seem different to others?
sitting in front of a balefire
i whisper to him uncertainly
are you a monster?
he looks at me
with his pure unguarded eyes
well that is for you to decide
he tells me

i take a deep breath as i ask
my next and final question
why do you only show me the good in you?
he smiles and says
why are you the only one who sees the good in me?
{*In love with a monster*}

is it normal
to feel so irrevocably in love.
{*Abnormal*}

how do i tell you?
we don't belong together
you look for peace in me
you look for the calm in me,
to the storm that is raging in you
how do i tell you?
i can't give you that
not because i don't want to
but because
i don't have that
i don't posses peace or calm in me
i have a hurricane of my own
brewing deep inside
all i can give you is my love
the love that consumes me
but that is all
my love for you burns bright
but not bright enough
to burn the demons inside me
they say love is strong
but is it enough
to be the rope that keeps us
from falling into our own infernos.
{*Is it enough?*}

swift glances from across the room
as we try to pretend
we don't know each other
as we pass in the hallway
no words are spoken either way
but there is something that lingers
a certain feeling
from the day we first met
we hid our love
reasoning that we weren't ready
that we weren't stable enough to be long term
but in the hallway
i catch the glimmer in your eyes
the one i see when you gaze at the sky
you grab my hand
and you pull me close
darting around the perimeter
to make sure we are alone
and as you kiss me softly
your lips pierce through the walls of my heart.
{*Paramour*}

if love means different things
for different people
then how do i know
what it means to me.
{*Meaning of love*}

i have known you all my life
seen you at your most humiliating
we have always walked together
through the highs and lows of life
yet as we stand together on this balcony
finally away from the troubles
of our restless lives
it's as if i truly see you
for the first time
your crystal blue eyes
common, yet unique in their own way
they shine whenever you talk,
about something you love dearly
i see how your face lights up
when you smile
remembering something funny
i see how you listen so intently
when i talk
how you gaze at me
when you think i'm not looking
how your body relaxes
when i'm in the same room as you
and finally i have an explanation
as to why i feel so different
when i'm around you
how my heart flutters
when you smile at me
how my breath hitches
when your hand brushes mine
i try to decipher

when i started to feel this way
but it’s hard to think of a time
when you didn't affect me like this
you're my serendipity
i wasn't looking for you
i wasn't expecting you
but god, am i glad i met you.
{*Skinny love*}

nothing is perfect
nobody is perfect
imperfections
they're beautiful.
{Perfection}

Angelicas

My life the way I chose it
The boy behind the mirror
The beauty of solitude
Happy never after
Middle
Oh great mirror
A difficult choice
Strength
My fire
The perfect girl next door
A thousand stories
Listen to me
I don't want to be numb
Holding on
No way out
The end of the tunnel

"People often seem to forget
freedom and hope can give us such great strength."

the day i was born as a girl
i became a prisoner to this crazy world
they turned me into their little puppet
they told me i was perfect, that they won't let me down
but they bullied me for smiling, and then ask why i frown
they said i could be whomever i choose
but my life had to be led by their views!
i wasn't allowed to be in love with anyone
and i could never have my own opinion
they told me that they deeply cared
they told me it was one life we all shared
they made me believe i was deeply loved
but a dark empty room was where i was shoved
they promise to stand by me everyday
but suddenly just left me astray
they said i wasn't allowed to cry
even if they told me a lie
they told me i carried their pride
i had to follow the rules till the day i died
they promised me they wouldn't deceive
but locked me up so i won't leave
i was told to love my body
they told me it was an angel that i embody
i couldn't be free like the others
i had to abide by the laws of our cultures
they made me feel like i was worthless
they rendered me completely powerless
they said i shouldn't make a sound
as they buried me alive into the ground
now... i shall rise again from my grave

it will be different this time because i am no more their slave
it is the resurrection of my soul
and my passion will keep on burning till the day i sail ashore
i see the world now in a different way
this time, those people will have to repay
it is my time to stop being hopeless
because i finally realize, i myself am a goddess
they can try and pull me back again
but i am not an animal that they need to train
i used to feel like i was trapped inside a cage
so now i can finally let out all that rage
so they might tell me i don't have a say
but guess what? i am also the one whom they pray
so the question now isn't who is going to let me?
now the question that comes up is who is going to stop me?
{*My life the way I chose it*}

the young boy looks in the mirror
in there he doesn't see himself
but, instead sees someone he does not know
he stares deep into the boy's eyes
it is in that moment the boy perceived
the rage and passion roaring in his soul
the boy in the mirror tries to move but can't
he thinks that he is not good enough
but he doesn't know that he is better than the rest
he needs someone to assist him
to show him the right direction
but the best guide for him
is the boy on the other side
people can bring you up or pull you down
you cannot control what they do or say
there is only one thing you can do
that is, believe in yourself
it is when you are going through
the most difficult chapter of your life
the hero inside you is revealed
and how beautiful it is when you finally realize
you have the strength to save yourself
faith is the boy's only key
to unlock this door of dread
to step across the mirror
and, live in the real world
because nothing can dim the light
that shines from within!
{*The boy behind the mirror*}

you can be around hundreds of people
but still feel alone
you can laugh and joke around
and yet feel broken on the inside
you might think you have longed for solitude
but somehow the loneliness does get to you
you get a feeling that's not sadness
but it is simply just the feeling of emptiness
you are the one who keeps all the others happy
but no one really knows if you're happy yourself
sometimes you think you want to disappear
but really, all you want is to be found
you need to learn to enjoy solitude
because in solitude the mind gains strength
and it learns to lean on itself
as whoever relishes solitude
is either a wild beast or god itself
being alone does not mean you are lonely
and being lonely does not mean you are alone.
{*The beauty of solitude*}

oh, honey you are such a princess
dressing pretty is the only quality you posses.
don't worry about the throne; it's your brother, who will be heir,
you cant be queen unless you have a king
your only hope to a happy life is a wedding ring
don't try to change the fabrication's design
no need for a fight it is all a plan of the divine
keep your body covered from head to toe
your body is the houses pride don't let it show
the men outside are like thirsty dogs
they will chase your blood, they are not afraid of any gods
the only way to stay safe is to follow our rules,
so stay at home and don't you dare talk to those fools
and that was what i did
behind their norms was where i hid
i tried to live my life by their demand
yet it didn't go as it was planned
cause they smelled the blood, oh…yes they did
i became an artefact on which they could bid
i tried to scream, but it felt like my head was underwater
i was called weak, like i was nothing more
than someone's daughter
i desperately wished it was a nightmare
but every touch felt like a new scare
when it stopped i felt like i was dead
cause i felt those ghosts and ghouls wrapping my head
i didn't want to fall asleep yet
but the last thing i saw was a distant sunset
from the burnt body you could only make out my hair

you felt so sad, you felt so sorry but all you could do was sit and stare
i see a light hoping to wake up from this nightmare
but it really did feel like they were all there
from up in heaven i see a time ages ago;
a women no one seemed to know
i wanted this all to be dream
i took time to realise i am not the old me
i could taste my own blood and it wasn't sweet
it felt like the rug had been pulled beneath my feet
i trusted their lies, i trusted those men
they broke me so much i couldn't pull myself back up again
was being burnt alive, no one could stop that pain
no one could save them either, they were already insane
i am gone now, gone forever
but don't you dare stop your endeavour.
show them you are not emotionally dead
make them hear every word you said
not one more tear to be shed
no more crying, start smiling instead
tell them you wont hear, even one more lie
now we break the cage, now we fly.
{*Happy never after*}

i'd rather prefer a happy middle
than a happy ending.
{*Middle*}

do not trust your mirror
for all it does is lie
it makes you think no one cares
about what lies on the inside
it only shows you what is skin deep
and not what lies underneath the covers
you can't see how your lashes fall
as you drift off to sleep
it never shows how the world sees you
when you're nothing but yourself
or how you just light up
when you're eyes are filled with love
it doesn't catch you smiling
when no one else can see you
your reflection doesn't tell you
how much you mean to me
so never trust the mirror
as it only shows your skin
and it can never dictate your worth
as it has never seen
the angel that lies within.
{*Oh great mirror*}

i stand here at a crossroads
bewildered between my heart and head
one way leads me to certainty
my mind tells me things my heart doesn't know yet
it feels like a storm is brewing inside me
the people inside my head are trying to kill me
the people inside my head are trying to save me
but i don't want to feel trapped inside my own head
i want to yell, to explore, to run and to be absolutely free
i glance away now to take a look at my heart
it shows me a way filled with endless possibilities
my heart knows things my mind just can't explain
it tells me to keep believing, to keep on dreaming
my heart questions the hard stuff, the rational thinking
my heart makes decisions that make me happy
i look clueless at both of them
it feels like the whole sky is on fire
i have made my choice now, and it is neither
i take the third road, the one not taken by many
i follow my heart but take my head along.
{*A difficult choice*}

not many people
can be as strong
as you are.
{*Strength*}

i have fire within
but just like the calm before the storm
like a deep breath before the plunge
i am waiting, waiting for the right moment
the very stroke of wind,
that will make the fire within me flourish
which will reflect the rage and passion
that lies within
i am here to prove to those who doubted me
to show them that i survived
because the fire within me burned brighter
than the fire around me
i will rise now
for it is the resurrection of my soul
the fire within me will burn day and night
till i sail ashore.

{*My fire*}

everyone loved her, the pretty girl
she was always so perfect
a fitted pastel pink dress
shoes to match, hair pulled back in a ponytail
not a single strand astray
she always said 'good morning'
a smile and wave to every passerby
never putting a toe out of line
not like the other girls
she wasn't 'a rebel without a cause'
she was 'the perfect girl next door'
her smile so deceiving
no one thought to look behind the curtains
no one saw the real her
the crescent moons carved into her palms
the tear stained cheeks hidden under foundation
the strands of hair she pulled at
the rough fingers at the back of her throat
as she emptied out her lunch
perfect
the word you'd use to describe her
the word she hated the most
why does she have to be perfect?
why does she have to look, feel & be a certain way
is it too bad to be different?
is it too bad if she likes the colour blue or black?
is it too bad if she wants to cut her hair short?
and wear boots instead of heels
what wrong does it do if she is a size 10 instead of 0
it doesn't hurt anyone if she is just herself

then why do we make her feel
so pressured to be someone else?
because trust me when i tell you this
the world would be such a great place
if we didn't fear the real her
if we stood by the woman she would become.
{*The perfect girl next door*}

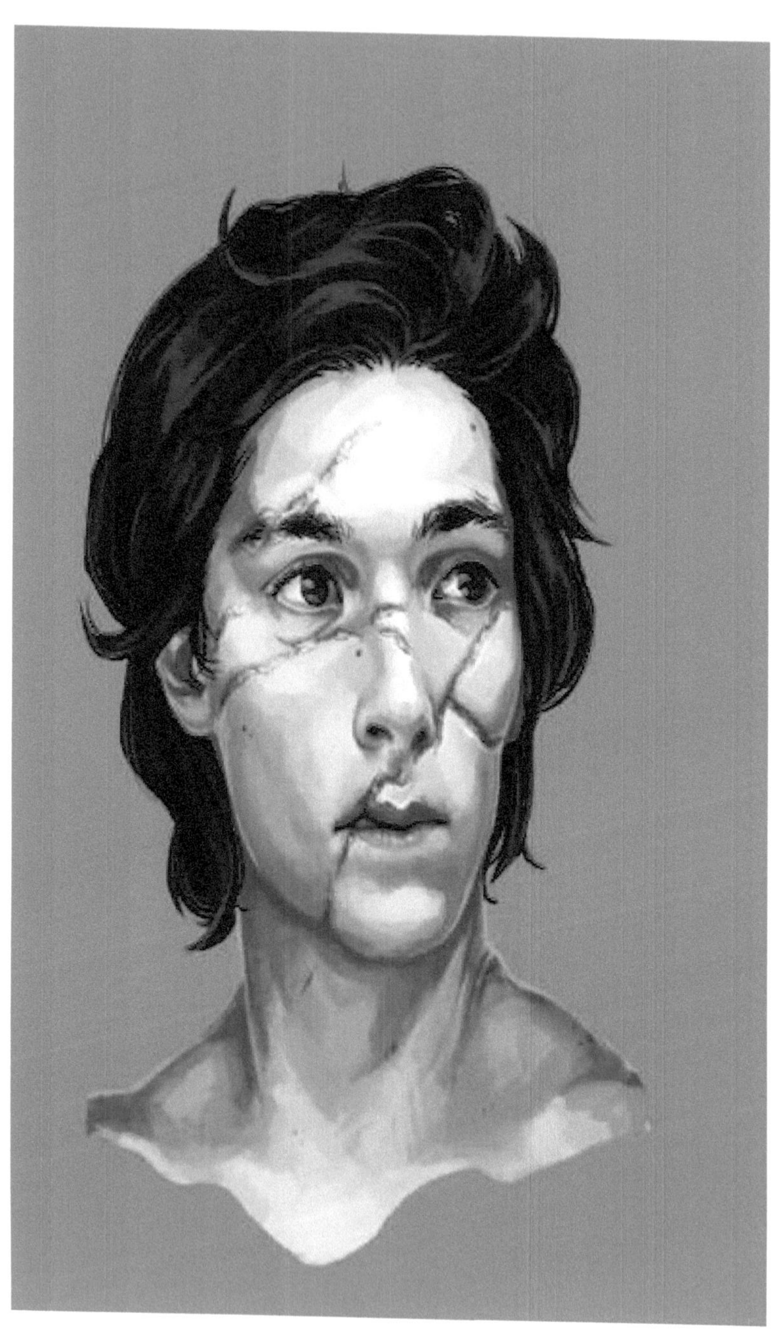

i tried to scratch them away
but they're still here
stuck to me like a perseverant shadow
i'm always tugging on my sleeves
layers of concealer to hide the secrets
i can't remember the last time
i looked into a mirror
and smiled at what i saw
i hate them

your scars are beautiful
i long to know the story behind each
i adore them
they show me how strong you are
the marks of a warrior
so let the world see
the ones on your arms, stomach, face
let them see the fighter you are
maybe not today
but one day, you'll love them too

maybe they aren't as bad
it hurts to remember how i got them
but i don't feel the pain anymore
some of them are fading
some promise to remain forever
i think i like that
the idea, they'll never leave me alone
maybe i'll skip the full sleeves today
and forget about the makeup
i guess, one day at a time
i can learn to love my scars.
{*A thousand stories*}

we are all so desperate to be
heard
we forget to listen.
{*Listen to me*}

"i don't want to feel sad anymore
i don't want to feel so angry
i don't want my heart to hurt anymore
i just wish....
i wish i could be numb"

do you really?
cause trust me you don't
you would hate it
yes, it does hurt right now
and maybe you want to scream
curse and yell at the world
but that hurt is what makes you human
the tears falling down your cheeks
the blood pouring from your wounds
they are the signs
signs that you're still alive
that there is still time
for things to get better one day
but becoming numb
takes it all away
a shell of a human
is all that's left
so talk , cry, shout
do whatever you want, just feel
because one day
the shouts of anger will turn to ones of glee
the tears of sadness will turn to ones of joy
and that frown will turn into a smile
then you'll realize
how it was all worth it, in the end

"maybe i don't want to be numb."
{I don't want to be numb}

as he handed me the glass
i took it assuming it was coke
as i took a sip i realised
the bitterness of the liquid
taken aback by the sudden tart taste
i felt like i needed to retch
but wasn't that how he was like
expecting a coke
being handed whiskey
expecting sugar
being given salt
expecting a gentle hand
but holding on to a rope
and as i pulled to get near him
tiring and difficult every time
it hurt
soon my fingers started to bleed
as i tried to hold on
hold on to something, anything
perhaps something that wasn't even there
until one day
when i could no longer hold on
and finally let go.
{*Holding on*}

i know things aren't great right now
there have been more
bad days than good
we haven't met in a while
our trip to the waterpark
got cancelled, instead
i'm at home watching
lame videos on the internet
no more late night drives
no unhealthy food truck dinners
instead i am in my pajamas all day
talking to you on face time
telling you, how in this time
i've read more
written more, especially
i've learnt something
when things seem to be falling apart
they might just be falling into place.
{*No way out*}

am i the only one
who can't fathom
that everything we do
will one day end in death.
{*The end of the tunnel*}

Lavenders

Hidden happiness

While it rained

Not enough

I wish my mind would slow down

My only friends

Fairytale

Goodbye

Winter is on my tongue

The wayward daughter

Anatomy of a writer

I'm not jealous

Falling fingers

Here lies my happiness

I am a poet

"When one focuses on the good
The good gets better."

i do not find happiness
the way others do,
how they are thrilled
at the most trivial things of life
oh, how they sicken me
a good night's sleep,
flowers to the sick,
floating in a pool,
the smile of a stranger
what lies under these gestures?
something i fail to see
it doesn't seem to bother me
i do not seek what others do
perhaps, because i want more,
i want to be loved
with a person's whole heart
i want to be set free
no limits to what i can do
i want to be remembered
for decades after me
not just by people who know me
but by strangers
i do not seek happiness
i don't see the world as others do
blinded by the lie of life,
i can see the truth
the truth of mortality
the truth of limited time
the others will never know this
as they might remain

high on this felicity,
till their last moments
when they accept the truth
with great perplexity
i shall not be so feeble
my mind is not flawed like theirs
but as i see them
in their last moments
and see very little difference
between them and i
they too seek for more
hiding behind those eyes
the loneliness, the fear is very evident
just needed to be searched for
i see it now
why they loved those things,
those seemingly meaningless things
the five seconds of happiness,
an escape from reality,
how even i am seeking happiness
i go out of my house
a stranger waves at me
i wave back
{*Hidden happiness*}

standing in the meadow, in her yellow summer dress,
barefooted, she could feel the wet grass under her feet
she let her hair down, letting the rain-wash over them
and she threw her hands up in the air
the droplets falling on every bit of her skin
her anguish hidden behind a mask
alas… she looked up at the sky and opened her eyes
this time she let go, let go of everything that held her back
she let the tears fall down her cheeks silently
she started to dance now, pushing all her sorrow away
she ran and ran till she was out of breath
and for just one moment the world around her
it all went silent
no one looked at her, no one knew who she was
all they knew, she was hushed,
like the wind blowing through their hair
cold, wet and drenched, she stood still now
forgotten, overlooked, neglected
just as the rose in her hand wilted and shrivelled
oh…how trapped she felt
she released her grip on the flower
and let the rain fall on her head
something had changed now
as she left that place
she couldn't remember the quite girl
all she could remember was the girl who laughed in the rain.
{*While it rained*}

i hate it
there are never enough words
to describe how happy you make me.
{*Not enough*}

i wish my mind would slow down
just for one second
enough for me to write down
the crazy things
that happen up there
the restless thoughts
that never seem to stop
those deranged ideas
too much to remember
if only i could write
the way i think
unbroken
fanatic
with an infuriating want
i would suffocate under
the ink flowing from my pen
i would breakdown at my words
and get up again as new ones come along
pages upon pages flowing down
like extremities into abysmal nothing
and i would write about
how everything in my mind leads to you
so i would write about you
a lot more than i ever could.
{*I wish my mind would slow down*}

they were back again today
calling me to them
wanting to talk to me,
the same way, i did them
my only friends
they always use to hide in the day
but came back out every night
coming out just at dusk
as they shone brightly,
through the infinite sky
we sit together all night
sharing our secrets
as they quietly listen
the night changes to day
dark changes to light
and they depart again
with a promise to return the next night
and so i bid goodbye
to my stars
to my only friends.
{*My only friends*}

if fairytales are nothing more
than mere stories
then darling, people will narrate
our lives to their kids.
{*Fairytale*}

why is it so hard?
to say that simple word
seven letters, one single word
goodbye
yet so arduous
the memories that come by
as the word forms in my mouth
an old lullaby
or a handmade sweater,
childhood secrets or
the last road trip
those fond memories
they leave us with,
tear stained cheeks
and sad smiles
as you near your departure
i try to hold on
looking at you like a lost child
i will miss you i say
with tears streaming down my face
you kiss my forehead
neither of us says the word
perhaps too scared,
to say them out loud
because after all
you were my favourite hello
and my hardest goodbye.
{*Goodbye*}

winter is on my tongue
as i speak in short, clipped sentences
autumn is in my eyes
they flash of gold in the light of a dying sun
summer is in my face
flushed with a sun kissed hue
spring is in my step
as i skip towards my fate
the seasons are in me
as i make my way home.
{*Winter is on my tongue*}

a wild spirit
with a soft heart
and such a sweet soul.
{*The wayward daughter*}

she has a typewriter in her brain
the people she meets, the places she goes
all turn to stories
with the click of those keys
her eyes are the gates
to the bookstore of her soul
not everyone can get in
but those who do
never seem to want to leave
a river flows from her mouth
as she speaks of her wildest fantasies
words strung together
in perfect harmony
as you are taken to a different world
ink runs through her veins
as she pens down her thoughts
every feeling, every emotion rests on a page
to be read even decades later
she has a bookshelf for a heart
some books gather dust
others being opened every day
every memory present there
some a single sentence
some an entire novel
she writes stories
about everyone she meets
with the sole hope
that one-day maybe
someone writes about her too.
{*Anatomy of a writer*}

stop saying you know how i feel
you truly don't
because i'm not jealous
it's not her that i strive to be
the only person i want
to be better than is me
so praise her, applaud her
put her picture up on the mantle
i'll be fine near the staircase
and you don't need to compare me
because i know how well she does
i too want to celebrate her
because she deserves it, every bit it
and i don't work hard because i want to beat her
i work hard so one day
someone, just one person will tell me
i'm good without adding 'you can do better'
one day someone might tell me
that i might not be as good as her
but i'm still worth it.
{*I'm not jealous*}

i want to write
till my fingers are numb.
{*Falling fingers*}

it is gone, but not forgotten
that's what she always told herself
years had passed
and the line turned out to be a lie
she walked past the grave again
unintentionally visiting those memories
she realized, she had forgotten
what he was like
how it felt
when he used to be here
how he made her smile and laugh
how he kept her content, in every moment
she missed how her life used to be
before he left, a long time ago
the pain resurfaces again
'here lies my happiness'.
{*Here lies my happiness*}

i'm a poet
and it gets hard sometimes
but given the choice
i would choose to write everyday.
{*I am a poet*}

Acknowledgements

Although I have written the poems in this book, there are many other hands that have helped the creation of it. Starting with my family.

My biggest thanks have to go to my mom; if it weren't for her support this book would never have happened. She has always believed in me, even when I myself have wanted to give up she was there to tell me how strong I am and how I am capable of achieving whatever I want. Along with being my supporter she has also been my biggest critic. She told me when my poems needed work or were plainly bad. And as much as I hated that it ultimately made my poems better.

To my dad, I hope he is proud of my work, I can never forget all the lessons he had taught me, and how he always knew that I could achieve great things in life. I remember the positive attitude and outlook he had on life and it is by adapting to that attitude I was able to keep going.

My grandmother and grandfather are two completely different people, but both are equally important in this journey. Dadi, she has to be the person who has spent the most physical time helping me, from making me a snack at any point of the day to cleaning up after me she has always made sure I had the perfect environment to work. Dadu, the sheer pride he has on even my tiniest achievements is a part of the reason why I keep working, the smile on his face and the pride in his voice when he tells others about my work is something I want to see forever.

Next comes my best friend, Kaashvi. She has always been and continues to be my hype man. There were times when she was even more excited than I to see my new work; her excitement was always like an adrenaline boost for me. She was the one person outside my family who showed me such support. Her constant reminder of "You are doing great." Helped me so very much.

All of my teachers, the ones who still teach me and the ones who I haven't had contacted with in a while, all deserve credit for helping me through this journey. It was one of my teachers who first read my poetry and encouraged me to put it out in the world. There have been so many English teachers over the years that have read my work and helped me in improving it. It is through their guidance and mentorship that I have improved in the past three years.

To every poet and writer out there, there are so many who have inspired my poems; it is by looking at their works that I was able to expand my horizon. Many quotes in this book are taken from the works of other poets or modified from their original form. And I am thankful for the mere existence of every writer in the world. You make the world such an interesting place.

And lastly, every single person that has supported me up to this point, my family members, my friends, cousins, teachers, and acquaintances. Even a single "Good job" or a pat on the back means so much to me.

www.ingramcontent.com/pod-product-compliance
Ingram Content Group UK Ltd.
Pitfield, Milton Keynes, MK11 3LW, UK
UKHW041844200726
13854UKWH00005BA/2056